Echoes from the Ball Park

Echoes from the Ball Park

A Brief History of Baseball

by Alan Ross

WALNUT GROVE PRESS
Nashville, TN 37211

ISBN 1-887655-86-7

Material for this book was obtained mostly from secondary sources, primarily print media. While every effort was made to ensure the accuracy of these sources, the accuracy cannot be guaranteed. For additions, deletions, corrections or clarifications in future editions of this text, please write WALNUT GROVE PRESS.

Printed in the United States of America
Cover Design: *Tal Howell Design*
Typesetting & Page Layout: *Sue Gerdes*
Cover Photo: Wrigley Field, *Allsport*
1 2 3 4 5 6 7 8 9 10 • 99 00 01 02 03

ACKNOWLEDGMENTS
The author gratefully acknowledges the friendship, deep support, and opportunity extended by Dr. Criswell Freeman. Thanks also to the magnificent staff at Walnut Grove Press and to Karol Cooper for her inspiration and dedicated contributions both during and between innings. A special acknowledgment to Navio Ottavi, my Little League coach in Wilton, Connecticut, whose sensitive diamond mentoring, I believe, made a difference.

For Bob
Whose kind, patient response to the endless,
insistent pleas of a little brother to play catch
was to reach, always, for his glove.

Table of Contents

Remembrance

It was my very first pickup game of baseball. And the ball field might as well have been Otsego Lake, New York, where the mythical seed of American baseball was first planted, for I'm sure it was no less crude: a raw, open pasture spotted with the occasional four-inch clump of hay-like grass.

One distinct memory from that afternoon on Liberty Street in Wilton, Connecticut, would stay with me all throughout Little League, right up to the time I was hit in the head by a Donny Temple fastball in my junior year of high school: *What senseless fool would willingly position himself in front of a screaming ground ball on a rough playing surface?* I'm still searching for the answer to that one.

For a time, I thought the sky was the limit for me in baseball. The Little League years had yielded some encouraging successes, including a no-hitter in my final season — the same year I led the Comet League with a .593 batting average and won the "Cy Young" award with a 5–0 record. But the game also brought me face to face with some real-life learning experiences — in particular, a tight game situation wherein I had my first true test of character.

It was in a game against the Bears, as a tiring, rail-thin eleven-year-old, that I found myself in trouble on the mound. They had loaded the bases and, clearly, I was getting rattled. Anyone who's ever been in a competitive situation knows that sickening feeling — *they're getting to me: I've got to dig in or bail out.* At that moment, my Little League coach, a kind and sensitive man, calmly walked out to the mound to settle me down. I was seconds away from throwing in the towel, and Coach Navio Ottavi could sense it.

Within moments my confidence was restored by Mr. Ottavi's renewed belief in me, and I retired the side. In a small post-game ceremony, he gave me the ball, simply saying I'd earned it. I still have that cherished memento, a gift from a man and a time I'll never forget. The faded pen inscription scrawled on the ball that day says:

> *Last game of 1956, won 4–2, two-hitter. Reason this ball given to me is because I didn't give up when the going was rough. I bore down like I hadn't during the other games. Mr. Ottavi thought this bit of confidence won me this ball.*

You can put me down as a fan for life.

A. R.

Introduction

Moe Berg, baseball's famous World War II spy who spoke 10 different languages, once remarked that it was his preference not to meet current ball players. Not that Berg, a 15-year major league infielder-catcher, didn't appreciate their work. It's just that he disliked having to "identify" his own credentials to *them*. He considered that to be, understandably, somewhat offensive — *I know you, but you've never heard of me*.

"Modern players think it all started with them," Berg contested. "Don't they know there were many of us here before they got here?"

Throughout my life, I've enjoyed learning the background of sports. Historical perspective somehow fits the experience of playing a game into a framework that carries more meaning than simply hitting, catching, throwing or fielding a ball.

It's about heroes and character, headlines and characters. It's embracing the great moments and performances that stand for a time and then are surpassed.

Inside these pages I've attempted to render my piecemeal song of baseball's history — echoes, if you will, on the olde game and some of its marvelous cast who created the collective soul of America's great national pastime.

Chapter 1

ORIGINS:
BASEBALL'S BEGINNINGS

In the Beginning

As the popular belief that Abner Doubleday invented the game of baseball wanes like the gibbous moon, Americans are living more comfortably with the game's probable beginnings. There was no single inventor; baseball evolved. Given these circumstances, it is no wonder that the game's roots are enshrouded in ghostly vagueness.

It would appear from the mountainous volumes written about baseball's origins that Dr. Daniel L. Adams, more than any other single individual, could be described as the true "father of baseball." Historically, Adams, an unsung major contributor but definitely *not* the game's founder, like Leo Durocher kicking up diamond dust, gave baseball a good kick in the pants down the road of the sport's ever-growing popularity.

Before Cooperstown

Baseball's first true historian, Henry Chadwick, cites the game's origins as emanating from the fourteenth century in England, then under the rule of Edward III. Youths of that period played a game called *bars* that featured running from one bar or barrier to another. The name, throughout the years, became corrupted to "base", and for a time, the barons of England in Parliament banned it as a traffic nuisance in the streets.

At some point, it was united with the game of *ball*, and formed the game of *rounders*, so-called because the players ran round a cyclical arrangement of bases.

Cricket Not Exactly "Cricket"

The English game of Cricket, also a ball and stick game, was a player on the board in America's efforts to institute a national pastime in the mid-1800s. But as the game's first genuine chronicler, Henry Chadwick, eloquently put it:

Americans do not care to dawdle over a sleep-inspiring game all through the heat of a June or July day. What they do, they want to do in a hurry. In base ball, all is lightning; every action is swift as a seabird's flight.

Eight Men Out

Before rules were standardized, baseball games ended when a team scored 21 or more runs or "aces," after both clubs had played the same number of innings. Also, the number of men on each side was not yet set, with eight men usually the norm. After the game, the victors would host the losers at a banquet.

The First Team of Influence

The New York Knickerbockers, formed on September 24, 1845, were the first team of real significance in baseball. The club's co-founder, Dr. Daniel Adams, was also involved in the early manufacturing of balls and bats.

"We had a great deal of trouble in getting balls made, and for six or seven years I made all the balls myself," Adams once said. "I found a Scotch saddler who showed me a good way to cover the balls with horsehide. I used to make the stuffing out of rubber cuttings, wound with yarn and then covered with the leather…It was not until 1858 that a shoemaker was found who was willing to make them for us. This was the beginning of base ball manufacturing."

The Knickerbockers consisted of lawyers, merchants, bank clerks, insurance agents, medical personnel, and "others who were at liberty after 3 o'clock in the afternoon," in Adams' own words. "Our playground was the Elysian Fields in Hoboken, a beautiful spot at that time, overlooking the Hudson, and reached by a pleasant path along the cliff."

Adams and his Knickerbockers would exist for almost 30 years.

The Knickerbockers' First Game

Though not the first game played in the New York area, the first official match played by the New York Knickerbockers took place on June 19, 1846, on the Elysian Fields in Hoboken, NJ. Their opponent that day, the New York Base Ball Club, smoked them by the score of 23–1.

The Knickerbockers, a conglomerate of 28 young men, named themselves after a volunteer fire company to which Alexander Cartwright (often mentioned, along with Doubleday, as the original inventor of baseball) and several of the Knickerbocker players belonged. Cartwright's involvement with the Knickerbockers, though deeply impassioned, was short — from 1845-1848.

National Association of Base Ball Players

In 1857, the New York clubs formed baseball's first association. Their aim was to standardize the playing rules of baseball and to regulate competition among the teams. At this convention, the bases were moved to a distance 90 feet apart from each other and the number of men to a side was set at nine.

Early Black Teams

According to the *New York Anglo-African* (December 10, 1859), and the *Brooklyn Eagle*, (October 17, 1862), at least four all-black baseball teams existed between 1859 and 1862.

First Ban of Black Players

The Ball Players' Chronicle, on December 19, 1867, noted that the 11th convention of the National Association of Base Ball Players voted unanimously "against the admission of any club (in this instance, the application of the Pythians of Philadelphia) which may be composed of one or more colored persons."

First Black in the Majors

Moses Fleetwood Walker, a catcher for the Toledo Blue Stockings of the American Association, was the first black player to make it to the majors. He and his brother, Weldy Walker, played briefly in 1884, before a wave of bigotry led by Chicago's Cap Anson ran them from the game. It would be over 60 years before another black man would play major league baseball — Jackie Robinson, in 1947, for the Brooklyn Dodgers.

First Professional Leagues

After the 1868 season, the National Association of Base Ball Players voted to recognize a separate professional division. But three years later, in 1871, the pros formed their own singular circuit — the National Association of Professional Base Ball Players. After five years, the league collapsed.

Its demise was directly attributable to an opportunistic stockholder with the association's Chicago club, William Hulbert, who proposed the formation of the National League in 1876. The new league doubled the existing park admissions fee to 50 cents and banned the sale of liquor at games. More critically, it signed its players to contracts that forbade them to play with any other clubs. Thus was born baseball's famous reserve clause that held players in virtual bondage to their teams for life.

Five years later, in 1881, a rival group at odds with the puritanical restrictions of the National League broke off and formed the American Association. They would successfully challenge the NL for the next decade.

The First Professional Baseball Team

On May 14, 1869, the first completely professional baseball team, the Cincinnati Red Stockings, formed by firebrand Harry Wright, began a winning streak of anywhere from 56 to 92 games (sources vary on the exact number of victories). But without a doubt, it was the Brooklyn Atlantics, on June 14, 1870, who finally snapped the Red Stockings incredible run, with an 11-inning 8–7 decision in Brooklyn. Twenty-thousand people crowded into the Capitoline Grounds for the event.

The game's outcome so devastated Cincinnatians that home attendance began to drop sharply. Soon, the team's investors withdrew their financial support. In short order, the Red Stockings were disbanded, whereupon the Cincinnati *Gazette* proclaimed, "The baseball mania has run its course. It has no future as a professional endeavor."

Albert Goodwill Spalding — Baseball's Messiah

As a young 17-year-old, Albert Spalding made headlines when he beat the famed Nationals of Washington, DC, while pitching for the tiny Forest City club of Rockford, Illinois. The finest pitcher of the 1870s, Spalding became the ace of the Boston Red Stockings, leading them to four straight championships before signing for bigger money with William Hulbert's National League paragons, the Chicago White Stockings. He would win 47 games for Chicago in the eight-team National League's inaugural season of 1876.

Soon after, Spalding forsook the playing field for a front-office spot with the White Stockings and assumed its presidency upon Hulbert's death in 1882. In addition, Spalding's own sporting goods business began to prosper, and he also published baseball's first official annual guidebook.

The Glove Catches On

The game was played barehanded until 1875 when, according to Albert Spalding, Charles C. Waite, a first baseman for Boston, began wearing a skin-tight, flesh-colored glove with a round opening in the back for ventilation. Spalding himself, in 1877, ventured out to the mound with a black kid-glove, and in 1883, Providence shortstop Arthur Irwin used one with the first known padding, to protect broken fingers. When New York shortstop John Montgomery Ward got wind of Irwin's glove, he and Irwin began showing it to other ball players, then eventually to a sporting goods firm. Within a year, almost every player in major league baseball had one.

The Curve

*I heard that this year we [at Harvard] won the
[baseball] championship because we have a
pitcher who has a fine curve ball. I am further
instructed that the purpose of the curve ball is to
deliberately deceive the batter. Harvard is not in the
business of teaching deception.*

— Charles W. Eliot,
president of Harvard University,
circa late 1860s

Candy Cummings, who pitched for the Brooklyn Excelsiors and later the Brooklyn Stars, displayed a curve ball for the first time in April of 1867. Purists of the game protested the curve as "unfair," but for Cummings "a surge of joy" overwhelmed him as batter after batter whiffed at his mysterious movement on the ball.

As he himself exclaimed: "Every time I was successful I could scarcely keep from dancing for pure joy. The secret was all mine. For a while, anyway."

Since overhand throwing was not legalized for pitchers until 1884, one wonders how Candy Cummings developed his devastating curve, first utilized in games, as historians note, back in 1867. Hmm…an underhand curve? Apparently so. Author Harry Grayson, in his book *They Played the Game,* mentions that Cummings "hurled in the underhand, cricket-bowling motion then in vogue."

Early Greats

Albert Spalding, the first man ever to win 200 games professionally, was teamed briefly on the field in the mid-1870s with the great Cap Anson, the Chicago White Stockings' superb first baseman and the first player to ever collect 3,000 career base hits.

Anson would assume a managerial role in addition to playing, in 1879, and at age 45, in his 27th year in the major leagues, batted .285. He led the White Stockings to five league championships in the 1880s.

Anson's teammate for seven seasons was perhaps baseball's first legitimate superstar — catcher-outfielder Mike "King" Kelly, a hell-raiser, brilliant base stealer and showman, who in 1887 was traded to Boston for the then-astronomical fee of $10,000. Both Anson and Kelly were known for their "kicking," a term that meant making trouble for others.

Another outstanding performer was Charles "Old Hoss" Radbourn, a tough right hander who won 60 of the Providence Grays' 84 victories in 1884. Against the New York Metropolitans of the American Association, at the end of that '84 season, in what some experts call the first "official" World Series, Radbourn won three straight games. In his 22 innings pitched during that championship series, his earned run average was a preposterous 0.00. In all, Radbourn amassed 311 victories in his career.

The American League

After 10 years of uncontested superiority as baseball's only major league, the National League began losing fans due to an increase in rowdyism and the lack of a season-ending championship series formerly supplied by the American Association.

Ex-sportscaster-turned-sportsman Ban Johnson announced there would be a change for the better, as he took on the National League monopoly by originating the American League in 1901. Former National League stars Cy Young, Napoleon Lajoie, John McGraw and others were lured to Johnson's new circuit, and by 1903, National League owners were eager for an agreement between the two leagues.

That same year, in the first postseason championship series between the two circuits, the Boston Red Sox (née Pilgrims, AL) stunned the Honus Wagner-led Pittsburgh Pirates for the world title.

Chapter 2

THE ALL-TIME NINE

An assignment of this magnitude is not for the timorous. Ultimately some paragon of monumental note is going to be stiffed. How can you leave out this legend, that immortal?

When you clench a sword between your teeth, you don't ask the person next to you for lip balm.

This mythical team for all the ages doesn't pander to time-tested stats or the safe consortium of others' opinions. It simply boils down to this: I am facing a *must*-win game. I want *these* nine guys on my team. Single-handedly, each can win me that game, offensively *and* defensively.

It is a brave yet absurd undertaking. But I like my chances. Here they are then — the nine greatest baseball players of all time, followed by the nine best at each position.

The All-Time Nine

Catcher	**Yogi Berra**
First Base	**Lou Gehrig**
Second Base	**Ryne Sandberg**
Third Base	**Mike Schmidt**
Shortstop	**Honus Wagner**
Left Field	**Stan Musial**
Center Field	**Willie Mays**
Right Field	**Babe Ruth**
Pitcher	**Walter Johnson**

Strange things happen to the reputations of players after they are retired. Yogi was always kind of a funny-looking little guy; he looked like if he was a piece of furniture you'd sand him off some. After he was retired, Joe Garagiola spent all those years telling funny stories about the kind of dopey stuff Yogi used to say and do. Gradually, the image of Yogi as a kind of short, knobby, comic-book reader grew larger and larger, and the memory of Yogi Berra as one hell of a catcher kind of drooped into the background.

Bill James,
historian-author

No one *feels* baseball better than Yogi Berra, no one relishes the excitement of its competition more, no one reacts more quickly to its constant challenge. He is a masterpiece of a ballplayer.

Robert W. Creamer

Catcher
Yogi Berra

Alias Lawrence Peter Berra. The New York Yankees' famous No. 8 (Bill Dickey's number as well) spreads some impressive data on the table. Yogi's three American League MVP awards cannot be minimized, nor his 18 All-Star Game appearances (including two games each in 1959, '60 and '61).

Berra had the good fortune to be a part of one of baseball's major dynasties: the Yankee teams of the late '40s through the middle '50s. But it's far more accurate to say he was the mainspring, the hub of those powerhouses. He anchored an almost unfathomable 10 world championship teams during his prolific 18-year career in New York. Later he would manage both the Yankees and the New York Mets.

Yogi gained a widespread notoriety for his own unique parlance of the English language — a sort of rootsy, homespun wisdom that has become a part of Americana.

A hustlin' ballplayer is a feller who never lets up for a minute, never gives his body a rest from trying. Lou Gehrig was the hustlinest ballplayer I ever saw, and I admired him for it. When I first saw him break in the line-up as a rookie, I went and told him just that.

Ty Cobb

Gehrig was the guy who hit all those home runs the year that Ruth broke the record.

Franklin P. Adams

A Gibraltar in cleats.

Jim Murray,
Los Angeles Times

G is for Gehrig,
The Pride of the Stadium;
His record pure gold,
His courage, pure radium.

Ogden Nash

First Base
Lou Gehrig

Baseball's Iron Horse needs no introduction to modern fans, thanks to the worldwide media hoopla surrounding Cal Ripken Jr.'s 1995 eclipsing of Gehrig's once-thought-to-be-invincible mark of playing in 2,130 consecutive games. But Gehrig's achievements go way beyond mere durability.

His offensive production would have garnered far more attention had he not played the majority of his career in the formidable shadow of Babe Ruth. As an example, Gehrig hit a home run immediately following the famous "called shot" home run of Ruth's in the 1932 World Series, but few remember it. He also outhit the Babe three home runs to two in the Series, but Ruth grabbed the headlines. Earlier that same year, at Philadelphia's Shibe Park, Gehrig smashed four home runs in a game — something Ruth never achieved — but it took a back seat to the news of John McGraw's retirement after managing the New York Giants for 33 years.

The two-time American League MVP, the "luckiest man on the face of the earth," succumbed, at age 37, to amyotrophic lateral sclerosis.

You could see the kid had a chance to make it. He had the body and he had the skills. I don't know if anyone knew he'd be this good. I think Ryne Sandberg just out-worked everyone.

Pete Rose

One day I thought he was one of the best players in the National League. The next day I think he's one of the best players I've ever seen. He's Baby Ruth.

Whitey Herzog,
St. Louis Cardinals manager,
on Sandberg, 1984

He made so few errors that when he made one you thought the world was coming to an end. Then he hits 30 or 40 homers and scores 100 runs. I saw them all . . . I saw all the best second basemen who ever played, and in my opinion Ryne Sandberg is the best second baseman who ever played baseball.

Don Zimmer,
former Chicago Cubs manager

Second Base
Ryne Sandberg

Up until the early 1980s, this race might have boiled down to a dead-even finish with Rogers Hornsby, Joe Morgan and Eddie Collins. But since then the Chicago Cub's Ryne Sandberg has rewritten the definition of a second baseman, with his showy offensive totals that indicate power (league-leading 40 home runs in 1990) and a consistency defensively that is unrivaled: No man in history ever won nine consecutive Gold Glove awards at the keystone spot. Morgan had five, and of course there was no such gauge in Hornsby's and Collins' day.

Ryno also holds the all-time mark for most chances by a second baseman without an error. In fact those 950 errorless chances better the record held at every position in the infield except first base.

Sandberg, a *Parade* high school All-America quarterback growing up in Spokane, Washington, was the National League MVP in 1984. He is a 10-time NL All-Star.

Mike Schmidt was one of my heroes. He had that short powerful swing, and his home runs looked effortless. He had style on the field and worked hard at the position. Just a tremendous all-around player.

Ryne Sandberg

I don't think I can get into my deep inner thoughts about hitting. It's like talking about religion.

Mike Schmidt

Third Base
Mike Schmidt

This three-time National League Most Valuable Player distinguished himself at a position that boasts formidable competition from the likes of Baltimore's Brooks Robinson and Kansas City's George Brett. Of course, B. Robby is everybody's all-time gloveman at any position, but Schmidt's outstanding fielding abilities are strongly endorsed by his own 10 Gold Glove awards, nine of them gained consecutively. He is also the major league's all-time leading home-run hitter for third basemen (509 of his 548 career total were accumulated while playing the Hot Corner).

Schmidt's peak moment during his 18 seasons likely came in the 1980 World Series, where his .381 batting average, two home runs and seven RBIs helped Philadelphia defeat Kansas City for the Phillies' first world championship in the 97-year history of the franchise. That same year he was named regular-season as well as World Series MVP.

Schmidt, a 10-time All-Star, once hit four home runs in a game (April 17, 1976, vs. Chicago), only the 10th player at the time ever to do so.

Every once in a while during fielding practice…a hush would come over the whole ball park, and every player on both teams would just stand there, like a bunch of little kids, and watch every move he made. I'll never forget it.

Paul Waner,
on Honus Wagner

He just ate the ball up with his big hands, like a scoop shovel, and when he threw it to first base you'd see pebbles and dirt and everything else fly-ing over there along with the ball. The greatest shortstop ever. The greatest everything ever.

Tommy Leach,
Pittsburgh Pirates third baseman
(1900 -1912, 1918)

Just pitch the ball and pray.

John McGraw,
to a young New York Giants pitcher
on how to pitch to Wagner

Shortstop
Honus Wagner

Over a hundred years after he first began playing in the National League, Wagner is still considered, by most baseball historians, the finest ever at his position.

Playing 18 seasons with the Pittsburgh Pirates during his 21-year major league career, Wagner claimed the league batting title eight times.

His burly physique didn't fit the prototype of the graceful, gazelle-like athlete usually associated with the shortstop position. The New York *American* once stated, "His movements have been likened to the gambols of a caracoling elephant." But his athleticism was unequaled, and he reportedly had the range of a Marty Marion and the instincts of a Lou Boudreau.

That he had good speed is evidenced by his five base-stealing titles. Wagner had a memorable face-off with Ty Cobb in the 1909 World Series, the only time the two greatest players of the early 1900s ever met. "The Flying Dutchman" outhit the renowned Cobb (.333 to .231) and even outstole the fleet Georgian, six bases to two, including a theft of home.

I just throw him my best stuff, then run over to back up third base.

Carl Erskine,
Brooklyn Dodgers pitcher, on
pitching to Stan Musial, 1948

Baseball's perfect warrior, baseball's perfect knight.

Ford Frick,
former commissioner of baseball,
on Musial

Left Field
Stan Musial

The greatest Cardinal of them all was one of the most steady producers in major league history.

Musial is one of only eight players ever to be crowned MVP three times. He also boasted surprising speed on the basepaths and a good if not great throwing arm. In fact, it is his defensive skills (he led National League outfielders in fielding three times) that give him the edge over the redoubtable Ted Williams for this all-time honor. His 24 All-Star appearances is unmatched by anyone. "The Man" claimed seven batting titles in his 22-year career, second only in NL history to Honus Wagner's eight crowns. His extraordinary evenness as a hitter is best shown by his home/away totals for base hits — 1,815 at home, 1,815 on the road. In a sheer slugging frenzy, he once belted five homers during a doubleheader on May 2, 1954.

Musial will always be remembered for his snake-like, coiled batting stance, about which former White Sox pitcher Ted Lyons once colorfully commented: "He looks like a kid peeking around the corner to see if the cops are coming."

I've seen Speaker, Cobb, Hooper — oh, all the great outfielders — but I've never seen anyone who was any better than Willie Mays.

> *Al Bridwell,*
> *New York Giants,*
> *four other teams, (1905-15)*

I'm foolish about Willie Mays. He is just full of intellectual energy. He kind of lets everything go for the end in view. Quite scientific and he certainly gets around the bases.

> *Marianne Moore,*
> *poet*

I went out early to see him in batting practice, and he hit about five balls in the upper deck. Then he went out in the outfield and he could just run like the wind and throw like hell. And I remember thinking this has got to be as good looking a baseball player as I ever saw. And it turned out he *was* the best player I ever saw.

> *Robin Roberts*

Center Field
Willie Mays

It's really not much of a stretch to call him the greatest baseball player ever. In fact, it is difficult to name a player of comparable hitting, fielding, throwing and running skills at *any* position, let alone center field. An injury-free Mantle or a speedier DiMaggio *might* have matched him.

Mays, a two-time National League MVP for the New York/San Francisco Giants and New York Mets, played in every All-Star Game from 1954 through 1973, and of course, is inextricably tied to one of the immortal moments in baseball history — The Catch, executed during the '54 World Series against Cleveland.

His 660 career home runs at one time was second only to Babe Ruth's 714. Some feel that Hank Aaron would have been chasing Mays' record instead of Ruth's had Mays not sacrificed nearly two years of his career to military service.

For those who saw him play, "The Say Hey Kid" left an indelible image: a bullet-like apparition, cap sailing off, flying along basepaths or corralling impossibly long fly balls. If anyone enjoyed playing the game more, they didn't show it more than Willie Mays.

I know one thing. Those balls Ruth hit got smaller quicker than anybody else's.

Walter Johnson,
on comparing home run hitters Lou Gehrig,
Jimmie Foxx, Hank Greenberg and Ruth

It wasn't just that he hit more home runs than anybody else, he hit them better, higher, farther, and with a more flamboyant flourish. Nobody could strike out like Babe Ruth. Nobody circled the bases with the same pigeon-toed majesty.

Red Smith,
The New York Times

He was a parade all by himself, a burst of dazzle and jingle…What Babe Ruth *is* comes down, one generation handing it to the next, as a national heirloom.

Jimmy Cannon,
New York Post

I swing big, with everything I've got. I hit big or I miss big. I like to live as big as I can.

Babe Ruth

Right Field
Babe Ruth

The man who "built" Yankee Stadium in 1923 used a bat rather than a bulldozer and is widely hailed as the greatest player of all time. That accolade more addresses his amazing versatility than the sheer raw slugging power which stunned onlookers for 22 seasons.

Ruth was also one of the best pitchers of his time in the mid-to-late 1910s. He won 23 games in 1916 and 24 in '17 during his six seasons as the hurling ace of the Boston Red Sox. Ruth's 1.75 ERA led the American League in 1916, and his World Series record for most consecutive scoreless innings pitched stood for 43 years.

But after the 1919 season, a near-bankrupt Red Sox franchise sold him to the New York Yankees, where a second, almost fiction-like career was launched. In 1921, Ruth ushered in the era of the home-run ball, with 59 round-trippers. That display is said to have "saved" the game of baseball which was badly floundering in the aftermath of the notorious Black Sox World Series-throwing scandal two years before. By the time he turned 26, Ruth had hit more home runs than any man in the history of the game.

Most people forget what a great pure hitter Ruth was. Though he's remembered more for his gargantuan home-run blasts, The Babe had a lofty career batting average of .342. His career-high .393 in 1923 incredibly failed to lead the league.

Surprisingly, "The Sultan of Swat" landed only one MVP award (1923).

I pitched against a lot of guys and saw a lot of guys throw, and I haven't seen one yet come close to as fast as he was.

> *Lefty Grove,*
> *on Walter Johnson*

You can't hit what you can't see.

> *Ping Bodie,*
> *New York Yankees (1918-21),*
> *on Walter Johnson*

On August 2, 1907, I encountered the most threatening sight I ever saw on a ball field. He was only a rookie, and we licked our lips as we warmed up...Evidently, the Nats had picked a rube out of the cornfields of the deepest bushes to pitch against us...The first time I faced him I watched him take that easy windup — and then something went past me that made me flinch. The thing just hissed with danger. We couldn't touch him...every one of us knew we'd met the most powerful arm ever turned loose in a ball park.

> *Ty Cobb,*
> *on Walter Johnson*

Pitcher
Walter Johnson

Long since he left the mound for the final time in 1927, Johnson's phenomenal pitching feats continue on in legend and lore. There are a handful of pitchers who ultimately have posted better numbers, but Johnson's achievements are all the more remarkable considering he hurled for most of his career with a cellar-dwelling or near-bottom club.

"The Big Train" recorded twelve 20-win seasons, including a league-high 36 in 1913, and his all-time strikeouts mark of 3,509 stood for 56 years until broken by Nolan Ryan. But for all his accomplishments, it looked like the magnificent Johnson would wind up his career without ever having pitched in a World Series.

Then, in 1924, the impossible happened: the Washington Senators won the American League pennant and went on to defeat the New York Giants in a thrilling seven-game World Series that went down to the final game in extra innings.

Johnson, then in his waning years and already a two-time loser in the '24 Series, came on in relief and heroically held on to win the game for the Senators, giving them their one and only world championship.

Historian Bill Deane once figured hypothetically that Johnson, a two-time league MVP, would have likely won seven Cy Young Awards during his 21-year career had the honor been bestowed back in his time.

Nine Best All-Time Catchers

1. Yogi Berra
2. Josh Gibson
3. Johnny Bench
4. Mickey Cochrane
5. Roy Campanella
6. Gabby Hartnett
7. Carlton Fisk
8. Ivan Rodriguez
9. Bill Dickey

Nine Best All-Time First Basemen

1. Lou Gehrig
2. George Sisler
3. Jimmie Foxx
4. Don Mattingly
5. Hank Greenberg
6. Eddie Murray
7. Keith Hernandez
8. Willie McCovey
9. Harmon Killebrew

Nine Best All-Time Second Basemen

1. Ryne Sandberg
2. Rogers Hornsby
3. Eddie Collins
4. Joe Morgan
5. Napoleon Lajoie
6. Bill Mazeroski
7. Nellie Fox
8. Roberto Alomar
9. Jackie Robinson

Nine Best All-Time Third Basemen

1. Mike Schmidt
2. Brooks Robinson
3. Eddie Mathews
4. George Brett
5. Jimmy Collins
6. Ken Boyer
7. Pie Traynor
8. Wade Boggs
9. Home Run Baker

Nine Best All-Time Shortstops

1. Honus Wagner
2. Ozzie Smith
3. Ernie Banks
4. Luis Aparicio
5. Lou Boudreau
6. Cal Ripken Jr.
7. Joe Cronin
8. John Henry Lloyd
9. Marty Marion

Nine Best All-Time Left Fielders

1. Stan Musial
2. Ted Williams
3. Barry Bonds
4. Carl Yastrzemski
5. Joe Jackson
6. Pete Rose
7. Ralph Kiner
8. Lou Brock
9. Joe "Ducky" Medwick

Nine Best All-Time Center Fielders

1. Willie Mays
2. Ken Griffey Jr.
3. Joe DiMaggio
4. Mickey Mantle
5. Ty Cobb
6. Oscar Charleston
7. Tris Speaker
8. Kirby Puckett
9. Duke Snider

Nine Best All-Time Right Fielders

1. Babe Ruth
2. Roberto Clemente
3. Henry Aaron
4. Frank Robinson
5. Al Kaline
6. Mel Ott
7. Tony Gwynn
8. Paul Waner
9. Reggie Jackson

Nine Best All-Time Right-Handed Pitchers

1. Walter Johnson
2. Nolan Ryan
3. Satchel Paige
4. Roger Clemens
5. Grover Cleveland Alexander
6. Bob Feller
7. Christy Mathewson
8. Bob Gibson
9. Greg Maddux

Nine Best All-Time Left-Handed Pitchers

1. Lefty Grove
2. Sandy Koufax
3. Steve Carlton
4. Whitey Ford
5. Warren Spahn
6. Carl Hubbell
7. Eddie Plank
8. Rube Waddell
9. Lefty Gomez

Chapter 3

The Nine Greatest World Series

The First World Series

The World Series had several "official" starts: in 1884, when the National League's Providence Grays defeated the New York Metropolitans of the American Association, and in 1903, when the American League champion Boston Pilgrims tripped the NL's Pittsburgh Pirates.

Actually, the very first World Series is considered unofficial: In the fall of 1882, the American Association champion Cincinnati Reds dodged a rule barring play between the National League and the AA by releasing all the club's players then re-signing them to separate World Series-only contracts. The Reds faced the National League's Chicago White Stockings in the first-ever world championship, but the results were anticlimactic: The clubs split a pair of shutouts.

No doubt rampant debate and perhaps some "kicking" will ensue, as old Cap Anson and Mike "King" Kelly might say, around the selections for the nine most classic of the Fall Classics.

9.

1934 — Cardinals Roll Behind Gashouse Gang

The rollicking Gashouse Gang of Pepper Martin, Frankie Frisch, Leo Durocher, Ducky Medwick, the Deans — Dizzy and Daffy — et al., win 20 of their last 25 games to edge out the Giants in the last weekend of the regular season for the National League pennant. In the World Series, they would face a daunting sluggers' row in the Detroit Tigers' Hank Greenberg, Mickey Cochrane and Charlie Gehringer.

The Series goes its entirety, the full seven, with the St. Louis Cardinals storming to an 11–0 shutout in the finale. The fabulous Deans account for all four Cardinal wins, splitting the victories evenly.

8.

1947 — Unknowns Star in Seven-Game Thriller

Big plays by "little" guys highlight this Series. In Game 4, the New York Yankees' Bill Bevens, a 7-13 pitcher during the regular season, is one out away from throwing the first no-hitter in World Series history, when Brooklyn Dodgers pinch hitter Cookie Lavagetto, who inspired the chant, "Lookie, lookie, lookie, here comes Cookie," lines a double to right field, scoring the two winning runs.

Two games later little Dodger left fielder Al Gionfriddo snags a potential three-run game-tying home run by Joe DiMaggio. The Dodgers hold on to win that game, but ultimately lose the Series.

Bevens, Lavagetto, and Gionfriddo, the trio of unknowns who rose to such heroic levels, oddly, never played another game in the majors.

7.

1926 —Alexander Turns Back the Clock. Cardinals Win First Crown

Considered washed-up at 39 years of age, the once-great Grover Cleveland Alexander had been a bargain pickup for the St. Louis Cardinals in midseason of 1926. Cleveland already had set the powerhouse New York Yankees down twice in the Series, including a complete-game win in Game 6.

Alexander, who fought epilepsy and alcoholism during his life, celebrated long, heartily and deservedly the night of his second victory. But the following day, with the score knotted and the bases full, with two out in the 7th inning of Game 7, Cardinals player-manager Rogers Hornsby nods to the bullpen for the old veteran.

What Alexander pulls off is legend: striking out rookie sensation Tony Lazzeri to end the threat with a masterful strategy of pitch placement. Alexander retires New York in the eighth but, with two out in the ninth, walks Babe Ruth. With back-to-back sluggers in Bob Meusel and Lou Gehrig coming up for the Yankees, Ruth inexplicably attempts to steal second. Catcher Bob O'Farrell, the NL MVP that year, throws Ruth out and the Series is over.

St. Louis has its first world championship.

The good Lord just couldn't bear to see such a fine fellow like Walter Johnson lose again.

Jack Bentley,
New York Giants losing pitcher in Game 7,
1924 World Series vs. Washington Senators

6.

1924 — Fitting Finale for the Big Train

At 36 years of age, it will likely be the last chance for the immortal Walter Johnson to ever win a World Series. The Washington Senators had just won their first pennant, but Johnson has lost his only two starts in the Series against the New York Giants. However, in the seventh and deciding game, Fate has stored a little something special up her magical sleeve.

The Senators tie the game in the bottom of the eighth on a bad-hop grounder over Giants third baseman Fred Lindstrom's head. In comes Johnson in relief in the ninth. For three innings, The Big Train holds up and holds on.

Finally, in the bottom of the 12th, a fluke play involving Giants catcher Hank Gowdy extends the at-bat of Washington's Muddy Ruel. Gowdy goes after Ruel's pop foul behind home plate, but the New York backstop inadvertently steps on his own tossed-away catcher's mask and fails to convert the play.

Given new life, Ruel strokes a double. Then, incredibly, another bad-hop single over Lindstrom's shoulder, this time off the bat of Earl McNeely, produces the winning run and the Senators' first and only world championship.

Most people are dead at my age. At the present time, at least.

70-year-old Casey Stengel,
after being fired by the New York Yankees
five days after New York lost the 1960 World Series in
seven games to the Pittsburgh Pirates

5.

1960 — Pirates, Mazeroski Overcome Yankees

One of the wildest Series ever. Never had there been such a monumental offensive display by a team who did not win. The New York Yankees accumulate a stunning total of stats: 91 hits, a Series-record 55 runs scored, bat .338 collectively, hit 10 home runs, and win three games by the scores of 16–3, 10–0, and 12–0.

Whitey Ford pitches both the shutouts for New York, but it still isn't enough to beat the scrappy Pittsburgh Pirates, who parlay a see-saw seventh game into their first world championship in 35 years.

It all ends on a bottom-of-the-ninth swing of the bat by Pirates second baseman Bill Mazeroski for a 10–9 Bucs win. Three different times the lead changes during the frenzied finale.

4.

1986 — Boston Boots Championship Chance

Just one out away from their first World Series title in 68 years, the Boston Red Sox find yet one more way to feel the Curse-of-Ruth legend that somehow keeps them from a world championship.

With a 2-and-2 count on the New York Mets' Mookie Wilson in the 10th inning of Game 6, veteran reliever Bob Stanley's wild pitch allows the tying run in from third. Wilson then hits a bouncer to Red Sox first baseman Bill Buckner for the apparent third out. But the ball stays low on the ground after two hops and rolls through Buckner's legs for the game-winning run, evening the Series at three games apiece.

In the decisive Game 7, the Mets rebound from a 3–0 deficit to take their second-ever world championship.

3.

1991 — The Worst-to-First Series

Both pennant winners, the American League's Minnesota Twins and the Atlanta Braves of the National League, had concluded their 1990 seasons in the cellar of their respective leagues. Both teams, though, jump to the top the following year, and their World Series showdown is regarded as one of the great classics.

Five of the seven games are decided by one run, and three of the contests are extra-inning affairs. Twins center fielder Kirby Puckett produces a defensive gem, robbing the Braves of a home run in Game 6, then winning the game himself with an electrifying homer in the 11th to send the Series to seven games.

Pitcher Jack Morris' masterful 10-inning shutout the following night gives the Twins their second World Series crown in four years.

October 4, 1955. Please don't interrupt, because you haven't heard this one before…honest. At precisely 4:45 p.m. today, in Yankee Stadium, off came the 52-year slur on the ability of the Dodgers to win a World Series.

> *Shirley Povich,*
> *Washington Post*

He never worried about running into the fence. That was the key thing.

> *Walter Alston,*
> *Brooklyn Dodgers manager,*
> *on the Series-saving catch*
> *by Sandy Amoros in Game 7*
> *of the 1955 World Series*

Ladies and gentlemen, the Brooklyn Dodgers are the champions of the world.

> *Vin Scully,*
> *Brooklyn Dodgers play-by-play announcer*

2.

1955 — Bums No More

They had played in seven previous World Series and seven times they had lost. Now, in their eighth Series, all even at three games apiece, the Brooklyn Dodgers put their hopes of vanquishing the mighty New York Yankees on the shoulders of pitcher Johnny Podres in Game 7. Center fielder Duke Snider has been the hitting star for the Dodgers with four homers, but it is a little-known left fielder named Sandy Amoros who makes the play of the Series.

With Brooklyn protecting a 2–0 lead in the sixth, the Yankees appear to be mounting a rally. Billy Martin and Gil McDougald both get aboard before Yankee catcher Yogi Berra comes to the plate, having already collected 10 hits in the Series to lead all batters. Berra's line drive slices toward the left field foul line and looks like a bases-clearing double at least. But Amoros, playing Berra towards center, races cross-country to the line to make an impossible catch, then quickly fires to relay man Pee Wee Reese, who throws to Gil Hodges at first to double-up McDougald. Podres blanks New York the rest of the way, and then it's Mardi Gras time in Flatbush.

1.

1975 — Big Red Machine
Stretched by Bosox

It's been called by some the greatest World Series ever. Supporting that contention are some strong facts: five of the seven games were one-run games; six of the seven were come-from-behind victories; and two were won in the ninth inning, while two were decided in extra innings.

The crown jewel of the Series is the unforgettable Game 6 — Boston's thrilling comeback win, attained by the joint big bats of Bernie Carbo and Carlton Fisk. Carbo's three-run pinch-hit home run in the bottom of the eighth ties the game, while Fisk's dramatic 11th inning "stay fair!" homer just inside the left field foul pole elevates the Boston Red Sox to an exhausting 7–6 win. Cincinnati's Big Red Machine, though, is too powerful in the end, taking the finale the next night on Joe Morgan's bloop single which gives the Reds the deciding run and the crown.

Chapter 4

BASEBALL'S NINE GREATEST MOMENTS

Like a feather caught in a vortex, Williams ran around the square of bases at the center of our beseeching, screaming. He ran...unsmiling, head down, as if our praise were a storm of rain to get out of. He didn't tip his cap. We chanted, "We want Ted." He did not come out. Other players begged him to come out and acknowledge us, but he never had and did not now. Gods do not answer letters.

John Updike,
on Ted Williams'
last at-bat home run

9.

The Kid's Final At Bat

The brilliant Ted Williams, called by many the finest hitter the game ever produced, has a list of accomplishments from here to Cooperstown: last man to hit over .400 (.406 in 1941), two-time Triple Crown winner, member of the elite 500 Home Run Club, six-time batting champion — all accomplished having missed almost five full seasons due to military service.

If ever there was a swan song to a career of note, Williams played it. In his final major league at-bat, against Baltimore on September 28, 1960, the Splendid Splinter wallops his 521st career home run. A farewell to remember.

It was the craziest curve ball I ever saw.

Tommy Henrich

I should have had it.

Mickey Owen

8.

Owen's Passed Ball Third Strike

One strike away from evening the 1941 World Series against the New York Yankees at two games apiece, Brooklyn Dodgers catcher Mickey Owen becomes the key figure in one of the biggest plays in diamond history.

With two out and a three-and-two count on Yankee right fielder Tommy Henrich, Dodgers pitcher Hugh Casey, who had mastered two completely different curve ball deliveries, fakes out his own catcher. Henrich swings at Casey's big roundhouse curve and misses. Strike three. Game over. But, no, the ball glances off Owen's mitt! Henrich races safely to first, and of course, the reprieve enables the Yankees to come back, taking the lead and the game with four runs in the top of the ninth.

New York goes on to beat the shell-shocked Dodgers the following day, closing out the Series four games to one.

7.

Vander Meer's Back-to-Back No-Hitters

The odds of it repeating are too astronomical to calculate: throwing consecutive no-hitters.

But on two June nights in 1938, it happens.

Pitching for the Cincinnati Reds, Johnny Vander Meer no-hits the Boston Bees at Crosley Field in Cincinnati on the 11th. Four days later, in the first night game ever at Ebbets Field in Brooklyn, the Dutch Master stuns the world with his second straight no-hitter.

An interesting side note: Fourteen years later, at age 37 and pitching for Tulsa in the minors' Texas League, Vander Meer hurls a 12–0 no-hitter. For the memories.

6.

Slaughter's Sprint from First

Matching wins one at a time with their Series rival, the St. Louis Cardinals enter the bottom of the eighth inning in the seventh game of the 1946 World Series against the Boston Red Sox, tied 3–3. Cards' right fielder Enos "Country" Slaughter hits a leadoff single. Two outs later, with Slaughter still stranded on first, Cards coaches give the hit-and-run. Harry Walker's "long" single to left center shotguns Slaughter on his historic dash. Rounding second and ignoring frantic signs by third-base coach Mike Gonzalez to slide, Slaughter, with a full head of steam, blows past third. Startled Red Sox relay man, shortstop Johnny Pesky, can't get off a solid throw to home. His errant heave brings the Red Sox catcher 10 feet up the third-base line from home plate.

Slaughter slides, fronting a majestic trail of dust, for the ultimate game- and Series-winning run.

I never say I have no-hit stuff. I know all it takes is one pitch.

Nolan Ryan

They just got in the way of a train.

Jeff Huson,
Texas Rangers shortstop,
on the Toronto Blue Jays' lineup
that went hitless against
Nolan Ryan, May 1, 1991

5.

Ryan's Seventh No-Hitter

At an age when, as pitcher Jimmy Key once put it, you hope you can still manage to pitch batting practice to your kids, 44-year-old flame-thrower Nolan Ryan of the Texas Rangers hurls the phenomenal seventh no-hitter of his fabled career.

On May 1, 1991, Ryan awakes slowly and in pain. Heating pads, Advil and a rubdown fail to alleviate the discomfort in his back. But that evening against the Toronto Blue Jays at Arlington Stadium, getting stronger as the evening wears on, the Ryan Express fans 16 batters, throwing a top-speed pitch of 96 mph to Joe Carter in the 4th inning and striking out Roberto Alomar to end the game with 93 mph smoke. Ryan fans five of the final 10 batters to achieve his milestone seventh no-hitter. No one else has thrown more than four.

To gain a better perspective of the consistent level of Ryan's dominance throughout his career, he also hurled a staggering 12 one-hitters.

4.

Mays in '54 — The Catch

Most observers of the game rate it as the greatest catch ever. Beyond that, it ranks as the greatest defensive play of all time: the stunning, impossible, deep center field catch at the Polo Grounds by the New York Giants' Willie Mays of Vic Wertz's seemingly endless line drive in the top of the eighth inning of the 1954 World Series opener against the Cleveland Indians.

Lost in the powerful image of the over-the-shoulder catch is Mays' whirlabout rifle throw to second base that allows only the minor movement of the lead Indians runner, Larry Doby, to tag from second and go to third.

Later, more heroics erupt for the Giants, who win the thriller on Dusty Rhodes' pinch-hit home run in the bottom of the 10th.

3.

Maris' Mega-Milestone

Of baseball's many milestones, this one may have been achieved under the most difficult and stressful conditions ever. Roger Maris was a man besieged and tormented during his phenomenal chase and ultimate surpassing of everybody's favorite baseball record — Babe Ruth's 60 home runs in 1927, accomplished in 154 games — 37 years before Mark McGwire's obliteration of the mark in 1998.

Maris' 61st homer, hit on the final day of the 162nd game of the 1961 season, brought controversy with it. Baseball's record book would only accord the feat separate, equal status alongside Ruth's record. Pressure-wise, Ruth's quest simply broke his own previous mark and wasn't comparable to the suffocation that surrounded Maris. Similarly, McGwire's astronomical assault was accrued without the pressure of a pennant race. Big Mac could aim for the fences on every swing, with his Cardinals 19 games and more off the pace during the season.

The Cards' PR staff ensured McGwire an orderly, sane exposure to the press. No such protection was accorded Maris. The Yankee slugger was left at the mercy of reporters for up to three hours after every game. Were it a diving competition, judges would be required to factor in Maris' "degree of difficulty."

The career and life of Roger Maris ended without full appreciation from baseball's public, who tended to remember him, until McGwire's ascent, more as a villain than as a great hero.

The Giants win the pennant! The Giants win the pennant! The Giants win the pennant!

> *Russ Hodges,*
> *New York Giants broadcaster,*
> *calling Bobby Thomson's famous shot*

Why did such a thing happen? It was just meant to be, I suppose.

> *Bobby Thomson*

If it hadn't been for that homer, who would remember Ralph Branca?

> *Ralph Branca*

We won't live long enough to see anything like it again.

> *Carl Hubbell*

2.

The Shot Heard 'Round the World

Overcoming a deflating 13-game deficit, the 1951 New York Giants go on a closing 37-7 tear in their last 44 games to tie the Brooklyn Dodgers and force a best-of-three playoff for the National League pennant.

With the playoffs tied at one win apiece, the Dodgers take a commanding three-run lead into the bottom of the ninth in the final game, on October 3rd, at the Polo Grounds. The Giants manage to push in one run before slugging third baseman Bobby Thomson steps up to the plate with two runners on. Dodgers manager Chuck Dressen then lifts his ace, Don Newcombe, for hard-throwing reliever Ralph Branca. On a one-strike pitch, Thomson hits an inside fast ball in an arc toward left field. It clears the Polo Grounds' high wall and settles just inside the lower deck.

The Giants, with one swing of the bat, had won the 1951 National League pennant.

Legendary sports journalist Red Smith eloquently states the magnitude of the moment for all the ages:

> *Now it is done. The story ends. And there is no way to tell it. The art of fiction is dead. Reality has strangled invention. Only the utterly impossible, the inexpressibly fantastic, can ever be plausible again.*

1.

Larsen's Perfect World Series Game

*The million-to-one shot came in. Hell froze over...
Don Larsen today pitched a no-hit, no-run...game in
a World Series...He did it with a tremendous assort-
ment of pitches...including a slow one that ought to
have been equipped with back-up lights.*

> — *Shirley Povich,*
> *Washington Post*

He was far from perfect, not even a lifetime .500
pitcher. But on October 8, 1956, at Yankee Stadium
in the fifth game of the World Series, the New York
Yankees' Don Larsen is total perfection: 27 Dodgers up, 27 Dodgers down. The event's place in baseball history is secured, the premier jewel in the Yankees 17th world championship crown.

During the game, in a serious breach of no-hitter
etiquette, Larsen approaches Mickey Mantle between innings and asks The Mick what he feels his
chances are of completing the no-hitter. Mantle,
horrified by Larsen's trampling of the time-honored
"don't talk about it" code, abruptly looks for some-
where else to sit. With Larsen in the zone of impec-
cability, Mantle needn't have bothered relocating.

Pinch hitter Dale Mitchell, the game's 8th all-
time hardest hitter to strike out, goes down on a
checked swing to end the game, and Larsen girds
himself for Yogi's bear hug.

Chapter 5

The NEGRO LEAGUES

No Favors

The American Negro wants no special class, no special place, no special street, no special trains, no special nothing. He wants to be regarded as an American citizen, with all the rights belonging to such. He asks no special favors and will be satisfied with none.

Associated Negro Press,
circa 1924

Nameless Faces

The lack of information about some of the "common" players of the Negro Leagues is one of the game's sad losses, historically.

A cutline from a 1920 photograph of Rube Foster's Chicago American Giants, the Negro National League's first champions, reads: *Standing (L to R): Christopher Torrienti, Tom Johnson, Unknown, Unknown, Rube Foster...*

When the big game shall have become history, there will stalk across the pages of the record a massive figure and its name will be Andrew Foster...The master of the show...the smooth-toned counselor of infinite wisdom and sober thought...Always the center of any crowd, the magnet attracting both the brains and the froth of humanity.

Sportswriter Rollo Wilson's
eulogy of Rube Foster

The Father of Negro Baseball

The dominant pitcher of the early 1900s, who coupled his natural talents for baseball with an entrepreneur's know-how, Rube Foster was an opportunist with the courage of a fighter. While continuing to pitch and manage, he took over his first administrative chores for the Leland Giants in 1910. Soon Foster was successfully raiding competitors for their top talent and building an awesome superteam. Those 1910 Leland Giants, renamed the Chicago American Giants the next year, went 123-6 and literally challenged the world, calling for a showdown with "all the so-called champions."

For the next decade, Foster stumped for an organized league. Finally, on Valentine's Day 1920, in Kansas City, Foster and representatives from seven other teams, including the Kansas City Monarchs, formed the Negro National League. He was named the first league president.

Sadly, Foster's mental and physical health began to fail in the mid-'20s, and when his American Giants, in 1926, claimed the World Series behind the clutch pitching of his younger half-brother, Willie, Foster was already in a mental institution.

He died four years later, at the age of 51.

Smokin'!

In a 1952 *Pittsburgh Courier* poll of ex-Negro Leaguers, "Smokey Joe" Williams was selected over Satchel Paige as the best all-time pitcher in the Negro Leagues. Williams pitched from 1897 to 1932.

Move Over, Nolan

Cannonball Dick Redding, a star right-hander in the 1910s and '20s, and a fierce rival of the great "Smokey Joe" Williams, reportedly threw 27 no-hitters during his celebrated career, including one against the major league Detroit Tigers in an exhibition in Cuba.

He makes Ty Cobb look like a runner with a handicap.

John Johnson,
Kansas City Call *sportswriter,*
on the running speed
of Oscar Charleston, 1921

Oscar Charleston

Considered one of the great impact players, Charleston exhibited a strong arm, raw speed and a big bat. An outfielder, he was called "greater than Ty Cobb or Babe Ruth" because he possessed superior defensive as well as offensive skills. Within the Negro Leagues themselves, he was likened to Josh Gibson as a slugger and to Cool Papa Bell as a fleet center fielder.

In his 21st season, in 1935, playing for the renowned Pittsburgh Crawfords, Charleston drilled a dramatic two-out, ninth-inning grand slam home run against the New York Cubans to lift the Crawfords to the Negro National League pennant.

The fastest man I have ever seen on the baseball diamond was Cool Papa Bell. He was on first base and the next batter hit a single to center. This fellow Bell by that time was rounding second base and watching me as he ran. He never stopped. As I started the throw (to third), I saw I was going to be too late. So I stopped. . .but he didn't. By the time I could get the ball away, he had slid into home plate, was dusting himself off and walking calmly away.

Paul Waner,
Pittsburgh Pirates
Hall of Famer, 1933

All these years, I've been looking for a player who could steal first base. I've found my man; his name is Cool Papa Bell.

C.I. Parsons,
Denver Post *sports editor*

The only comparison I can give is — suppose Willie Mays had never had a chance to play big league. Then I were to come to you and try to tell you about Willie Mays. Now this is the way it is with Cool Papa Bell.

Monte Irvin

Speed Cools

The story is familiar to many now. Legendary speed. So fast that he could flick the lights off and be in bed before the room goes dark. The gratuitous quotes on the previous page don't sound like anything less than the stuff of which true legends are made.

James "Cool Papa" Bell began playing professionally in 1922 and was still playing 25 years later when Jackie Robinson took the big leap. Bell's cloud-of-dust speed soon earned him the title of black baseball's swiftest man.

"Bell is somewhat of a hoofer," once commented Dizzy Dismukes, a former Indianapolis ABCs ace right-hander in the mid- to late-1910s and later a writer, scout, and baseball executive.

Like many of the Negro League stars, Bell went south to Cuba and Mexico to play winter league ball, often joining Satchel Paige's barnstorming junkets as well.

The man who could outrace any fly ball may have been the world's fastest human at the time, too. Sprinter Jesse Owens, the 1932 Olympic Games four-time gold medalist, regularly raced major league baseball's fastest men in exhibitions and dispatched them easily. But he somehow always managed to successfully dodge any head-to-head matchups with Bell, often citing the absence of his track shoes as a reason for passing up the challenge.

This big guy, Josh Gibson...he is one of the greatest backstops in history, I think.

Carl Hubbell

He hits the ball a mile. Throws like a rifle. Bill Dickey isn't as good a catcher.

Walter Johnson,
on Josh Gibson

Josh Gibson was, at the minimum, two Yogi Berras.

Bill Veeck

I don't break bats, I wear 'em out.

Josh Gibson

Josh Gibson

Gibson was called "the black Babe Ruth", but many observers of the legendary slugger from the Negro Leagues era felt that Ruth should've been called "the white Josh Gibson."

In 1931, Gibson is reported to have slammed in excess of 70 home runs, counting both league, non-league and winter-league games. Though definitive statistics are minimal from the Negro Leagues, Gibson likely amassed between 800 and 1,000 home runs during his 15-year professional baseball career. His ten homers hit at Griffith Stadium in Washington, DC, in 1943, was a single-season stadium record.

His flame was brilliant, but short. At age 36, the year Jackie Robinson and not Josh Gibson broke baseball's longtime color line, Gibson died.

You know, my fast ball looks like a change of pace alongside that little pistol bullet ol' Satch shoots up to the plate.

Dizzy Dean,
1935

The prewar Paige was the best pitcher I ever saw.

Bob Feller

He was the toughest pitcher I ever faced.

Joe DiMaggio

People came from miles around to see him. He was the biggest name in the game. He was like Babe Ruth. He had charisma; he had that hesitation pitch, that windmill wind-up...

Monte Irvin

All the years I played, I never got a hit off him. He threw *fire*. That's what he threw.

Buck Leonard

The Satchel Tree

Born Leroy Paige, on July 7, 1906, in Mobile, Alabama, the legendary Satchel Paige is considered the best known and certainly biggest star in the history of the Negro Leagues. His pro career began in 1926 and ended in 1965 — a 40-year span. His fast ball was so unhittable that he didn't develop a curve ball until the mid-1930s. His nickname came from a boyhood job carrying bags at a railway station. To transport several of them at a time, he slung a pole across his shoulders, placing the bags along it. A friend said he "looked like a walking satchel tree."

It wasn't till 1948 that Paige finally got a chance (with Cleveland) to show his legendary pitching form in the newly integrated major leagues. He was then 42. His heyday achievements will never completely be statistically supported, but it is estimated Paige appeared in close to 2,600 ball games, hurling in the vicinity of 300 shutouts, with a headshaking 55 no-hitters.

Paige is considered in the same breath with the great Walter Johnson as one of the top pitchers of all time. He had a journeyman's career, barnstorming and team-hopping with a number of mixed teams in his prime. His most notable years were with the Pittsburgh Crawfords and the Kansas City Monarchs.

East-West Game

Gus Greenlee, founder of the second Negro National League in 1933, originated, along with *Pittsburgh Sun-Telegram* employee Roy Sparrow, the East-West Game. Debuting the same year as the major league All-Star Game (1933), the East-West became an instant classic and was the centerpiece for black baseball through the mid-1940s. The inaugural game drew 20,000 to Chicago's Comiskey Park. Ultimately it would average upward to 30,000 in attendance.

Exhibitions vs. Major Leaguers

Many games between all-black teams and major league all-stars took place during the Negro League years, particularly in the off-season for both.

Of the 438 known exhibitions that occurred, black teams won 309 of them.

Negro Leaguers in Cooperstown

- **Satchel Paige** (inducted in 1971)
- **Josh Gibson** (1972)
- **Buck Leonard** (1972)
- **Monte Irvin** (1973)
- **James "Cool Papa" Bell** (1974)
- **Judy Johnson** (1975)
- **Oscar Charleston** (1976)
- **John Henry Lloyd** (1976)
- **Martin DiHigo** (1977)
- **Rube Foster** (1980)
- **Ray Dandridge** (1987)
- **Leon Day** (1995)
- **Bill Foster** (1996)
- **"Bullet" Joe Rogan** (1998)

The essence of Negro baseball died in the fall of 1945, when Jackie Robinson signed his historic contract with the Montreal Royals...(The Negro Leagues') eventual passing prompted no elegies, no mourning. (They) were designed to provide opportunity where opportunity was denied and to offer vibrant proof that there was no legitimate basis for the major leagues' unwritten rule. Their death was their ultimate victory.

Phil Dixon, Patrick J. Hannigan,
The Negro Baseball Leagues

Chapter 6

NINE EPIC MILESTONES

511

Everybody knows Cy Young is the winningest pitcher in major league history, with 511 victories. What some people may not know is that he is also the losingest pitcher of all time, with 316 losses.

Young broke into the majors as a sensation in August of 1890. In his debut, he humbled the Chicago White Stockings and their vocally obnoxious manager and star, Cap Anson, allowing just three hits. Young's dominating impact, along with that of the New York Giants' Amos Rusie, was so profound it has been said the pitching mound was moved back to its current distance of 60 feet, 6 inches from home plate to better balance the duel between pitcher and batter.

Young's sterling career spanned 22 seasons: most notably with Cleveland (then in the National League) for nine campaigns and eight with Boston in the American League.

4,192

I will never say I was a better baseball player than Cobb. All I'll say is I got more hits than he did.
— Pete Rose

Breaking an epic major league record is all the more meaningful when the previous record-holder happens to be a giant of the game — Ruth surpassed by Maris and Aaron, Gehrig by Ripken, Johnson by Ryan. . .and the one and only Ty Cobb by Pete Rose. Soldering season upon season (ten 200-hit seasons) for 24 years brings Rose into the sacred presence of Cobb and his career total hits mark.

On a night tailor-made for worship from 47,237 adoring Riverfront fans in Cincinnati, Rose lines a single to left-center field off San Diego's Eric Show to record his 4,192nd base hit.

The date itself carries its own significance: fifty-seven years ago to the very night, Cobb concluded his incomparable major league career. The fact that it takes him nearly 2,000 more at-bats than the Georgia Peach to surpass the record only affords Rose a great opportunity for a respectful comment (see above).

I reckon it might have been safer to throw behind him. I don't guess Ruth hit those behind his head much better than the next guy.

Tom Zachary,
Washington Senators pitcher
who served up Babe Ruth's 60th home run
in 1927

60

The larger-than-life, legendary Babe Ruth raised the bar on his own existing season home run mark, on September 30, 1927, at Yankee Stadium against the Washington Senators' Tom Zachary. Ruth's right field bleachers smash comes, dramatically enough, in the bottom of the eighth, with the score tied 2-2.

All but forgotten in the magnitude of Ruth's landmark event is the appearance of the Senator's Big Train for 21 seasons, Walter Johnson, as a pinch hitter in the top of the ninth for Washington. It would be the last curtain call of his brilliant career.

Wherever my old teammate Lou Gehrig is today, I'm sure he's tipping his cap to you, Cal Ripken.

Joe DiMaggio

This is the closest thing to an out-of-body experience I'll ever have.

Cal Ripken Jr.

2,131

It takes an iron will as well as an iron man to overtake an Iron Horse. But on the night of September 6, 1995, in the comfort of Camden Yards, Baltimore's eternal Oriole, Cal Ripken Jr., having played more than 13 seasons in a row without missing a single game, steps ahead of another immortal's timeless feat: Lou Gehrig's seemingly unbreakable record of 2,130 consecutive games played.

Prior to Ripken, no one has even come within five years of the mark. A 22-minute, 15-second standing ovation from the crowd salutes his achievement. In true Hollywood fashion, Ripken hits home runs on each of the evenings in which he ties, then breaks, Gehrig's great standard — crowning, punctuating statements for such an historic occasion.

Three years later, on the night of September 20, 1998, after 16 seasons of continuous play, Ripken voluntarily elects to sit one out, ironically against the New York Yankees, Gehrig's old team. As the significance of the moment floods Camden Yards, the Yankees en masse leap from the dugout, tipping their caps in tribute to baseball's infinite Iron Man.

I'm not trying to break any record of Babe Ruth. I'm just trying to make one of my own.

Hank Aaron

715

It was one of those marks that, in everyone's mind, seemed invincible. Numbers have a strange way of anesthetizing you when they're used effectively. Babe Ruth's 714 lifetime home runs was a number as difficult to fathom as earth's distance from the sun, 93,000,000 miles.

Hank Aaron, to his advantage, kind of snuck up on the record, quietly accumulating blast after blast till he had 600 of them. Then people started to turn their undivided attention to him, and the mounting pressure and media circus began. Handling it all with a magnificent grace, Aaron, on the night of April 8, 1974, against Los Angeles Dodgers left-hander Al Downing, slams the record 715th home run of his superlative career.

He would go on to hit 40 more, leaving baseball's most famous milepost, well, about 93,000,000 miles from any future pretenders to the throne of all-time home run king.

Clemens Fans 20 — Twice

In his first full season with Boston, in 1986, young Roger Clemens goes to work against Seattle early in the season and serves nationwide notice that The Rocket is officially lit. Through four innings, Clemens sits down nine Mariners via strikeouts. Sixteen is the total after seven. In the ninth, with his strikeout number standing at 18, Clemens smokes the first two batters, and suddenly one of baseball's most esteemed records is in his mitt.

Lightning of the rarest kind strikes 10 years later. On the cold night of September 18, 1996, Clemens' staggering feat is tied — by Clemens again! This time, the assault, against the Detroit Tigers, is all the more spectacular, all the more improbable because of The Rocket's age. Though Chicago Cubs rookie phenom Kerry Wood ties the mark in May of 1998, Clemens' K-mark double remains one of the game's enduring feats.

In 1998, at age 36, Clemens rocks the baseball world when he picks up his fifth Cy Young Award, unprecedented in baseball history and assuring him a spot among the game's immortals.

56

It may be the most celebrated sports achievement of all time: Roger Bannister's four-minute mile, Bobby Jones' Grand Slam, and Johnny Unitas' 47-game TD pass mark all in one. From May 15 through July 17, 1941, New York Yankees center fielder Joe DiMaggio hits safely in 56 straight games. For oddities, The Yankee Clipper immediately begins another hit streak that goes 16 games before coming to an end. As an 18-year-old minor leaguer with the San Francisco Seals, in 1933, he had set a phenomenal 61-game consecutive hit streak.

During DiMaggio's torrid two-month tear that sets the big-league mark, he bats .408 and collects 91 hits, with 22 multiple-hit games. More importantly from Joltin' Joe's standpoint, the Yankees go 41–13 (with two ties) during the interlude.

I think the magnitude of the number won't be understood for a while. I mean, it's unheard of for somebody to hit 70 home runs. So, I'm like in awe of myself right now.

Mark McGwire

If somebody wants to call him a failure, stand up and call it, and have your house burned, have your children kidnapped.

Tony La Russa,
St. Louis Cardinals manager

The home run *is* America — appealing to its roots of rugged individualism and its fascination with grand scale. Americans gape at McGwire's blasts the same way they do at Mount Rushmore, Hoover Dam and the Empire State Building.

Tom Verducci,
writer, CNN/Sports Illustrated

70

History's perspective only has a way of gaining clarity over time itself. While there is no denying the prodigious nature of Mark McGwire's staggering 70-home run season in 1998, it will be difficult to assess its relativity within baseball's hallowed annals for some time yet. Who's to say that Ken Griffey Jr. won't go out and hit 72 home runs next year? McGwire has already said he won't attempt to break his own record. On the surface, the player most motivated to go after it would appear to be Sammy Sosa. Before his magnificent 1998 season, Sosa, not unlike Roger Maris, had not previously been regarded by the game's observers as a legitimate pretender to the home run crown.

What brought venerableness to Maris' feat was that it stood up against the onslaught of baseball's best for 37 years. In addition, Big Mac had the support of all America behind him. Maris was cast as an unworthy usurper — the man who would dethrone the most popular hero in the history of American sport. Even among Yankee fans, Maris was not the favorite. In 1961, Mickey Mantle played the role of Sosa, giving laudable chase to Maris' run to infamy.

Be all that as it may, the game's new Superman is indeed adorned in red and blue. To you, Mark McGwire, we tip our cap.

Jackie Takes the Field

The greatest untapped reservoir of raw talent in the history of the game is the black race. The Negroes will make us winners for years to come. And for that I will bear happily being called a bleeding heart and a do-gooder.

— Branch Rickey,
1945

To do what Jackie did has got be the most tremendous thing I've ever seen in sports.

— Pee Wee Reese

With the weight on his young shoulders of thousands of players who never were allowed the opportunity to play in white baseball's major league, coupled with the additional burden of carrying his race's color flag for all, Jackie Robinson steps out onto Ebbets Field, on April 15, 1947, to play first base for the Brooklyn Dodgers — major league baseball's first black player in over 60 years.

Enduring an endless season-long assault of denigrating abuse, Robinson goes on to hit .297, lead the league in stolen bases (29) and win Rookie of the Year honors.

Chapter 7

THE NINE BEST OLD BALL PARKS

Ball Park Boom

The big boom in ball park construction came prior to World War I. More often than not, these were inner-city parks and had to configure to the particular constraints of the surrounding neighborhood. It wasn't uncommon to see these monolithic steel-and-concrete fortresses wedged in, in shoehorn fashion, between oddly angled avenues and streets. Between 1900 and 1915 the following parks sprang up or were entirely renovated:

- Forbes Field (Pittsburgh)
- Ebbets Field (Brooklyn)
- Crosley (née Redlands) Field (Cincinnati)
- Braves Field (Boston)
- Polo Grounds (New York)
- Sportsman's Park (St. Louis)
- Wrigley Field and Comiskey Park (Chicago)
- Tiger Stadium (née Briggs, née Navin Field, née Bennett Park — Detroit)
- Griffith Stadium (Washington, DC)
- Shibe Park (Philadelphia)
- League Park (Cleveland)

After Yankee Stadium was completed in 1923, no new ball parks would be built for 30 years (County Stadium, Milwaukee, 1953).

Long Gone, Lovable, Quirky Nooks and Crannies

Braves Field, Boston — Center field marker at one time was 550 feet from home plate.

Crosley Field, Cincinnati — Three-foot sloping incline in left field to the left field wall.

Ebbets Field, Brooklyn — Right field wall was concrete and concave with a screen on top. Depending on which part of the wall it hit, a ball could bounce back toward the infield, straight up in the air, or if it hit the screen, drop straight down.

Forbes Field, Pittsburgh — Covered box seats on top of the grandstand, from behind first base all the way around to third: baseball's first sky boxes.

Tiger Stadium, Detroit — Its right field upper deck overhangs the lower by 10 feet. A peculiar feature of the park: Home plate and the batters' boxes are not in alignment with the pitcher's mound but face slightly toward right-center field.

Griffith Stadium, Washington, DC — The fence in right-center field took an irregular turn to dodge the property of landowners reluctant to accommodate the stadium.

League Park, Cleveland — a 375-foot left field foul line and a bleacher wall in left center that had four little three-step stoops leading directly down onto the playing field and were in the field of play.

Polo Grounds, New York — Only 279 feet down the left field foul line and just 257 feet down the right, the concrete outfield walls shot straight out from the foul poles, parallel to the home plate-pitcher's mound line. In deepest center field, in fair territory, 483 feet from home plate, was a monument to Captain Eddie Grant — an ex-Giant and the first major leaguer killed in World War I.

9.

Sportsman's Park

Home to both the St. Louis Browns (1909-1953) and the Cardinals (1920-1966), Sportsman's Park's playing field was rotated during its major reconstruction in 1909. The old home-plate area became left field, while the new home plate was anchored in the southwest Spring Ave.-Dodier St. corner of the park.

Looking straight down the left field foul line, the massive double-decked grandstand looked like it had been sliced off with a gigantic saw right at the foul pole.

In 1929, an infamous 33-foot high screen was erected atop the 11½-foot solid concrete wall in right field. With the exception of the 1955 season, it remained until the park's demise in 1966 — a virtual singing-sirens net where home-run hopes were regularly dashed. It was also the last segregated seating area in a major league ball park. That practice was finally abolished in early 1944.

Many immortal moments haunt the park, including Bill Veeck's pinch-hitting midget stunt in 1951 and Enos Slaughter's mad scoring dash from first on a single to win the 1946 World Series. It was also the setting for the "Street Car Series" in 1944 — St. Louis' only intercity World Series. The Cardinals won, four games to two.

8.
Tiger Stadium

Operating on the theory that an old live ball park is better than an old dead one, I've elected to salute the three "living" old fortresses from yesteryear in my Nine Best — Fenway, Wrigley and Tiger. The choice to honor them I'm sure puts me contrary with supporters of Comiskey Park, Forbes Field, Griffith Stadium and Braves Field among others — all of which would legitimately vie for a spot.

Leading off for Detroit is an impressive historical fact: The site of Trumball and Michigan Avenues remains the oldest continuous location of major league baseball in existence. Having originated as Bennett Park in 1896, the venue hosted the debut of one of the game's most significant contributors — Ty Cobb. It was renamed Navin Field in 1912 before again changing names, this time to Briggs Stadium in 1938. It became Tiger Stadium in 1961.

The kinder-gentler set will appreciate knowing that it is the only ball park ever to be hugged: twice in fact — in 1988 and 1990 — as a show of support from Stadium preservationists.

It has housed its share of major events, including 14 of Denny McLain's 31 wins in 1968. The future for Tiger Stadium is uncertain. While hoping the preservationists win their battle, will the city maintain the venue after the Tigers leave in the year 2,000?

The trick was to plant yourself about three feet from the incline and then, when you broke back, you counted those three steps to yourself. If you didn't, you'd stumble and fall every time.

Ralph Kiner,
on Crosley Field's
notorious left field incline

7.

Crosley Field

Cincinnati's Crosley Field offered a cornucopia of endearing aberrations during its 58-year run that began in 1912.

The most widely debated and historic feature of the park was its notorious left field "terrace," which gradually inclined three feet to the wall. It was the bane of many a visiting left fielder, and no less a figure than Babe Ruth was humiliated by it.

The major league's first night game was played at Crosley, on May 24, 1935. A nostalgic signpost for fans adorned the top of a building beyond the left-center field wall: HIT THIS SIGN AND GET A SIEBLER SUIT. Longtime Reds outfielder Wally Post was fitted for 16 of them over the course of his career.

When an Ohio River tributary, the Millcreek, overflowed in January 1937, Crosley Field went under 21 feet of water. A famous photo shows Reds pitcher Lee Grissom in a rowboat out beyond second base. He eventually rowed *over* the wall in left field!

Other Crosley milestones include the first of Johnny Vander Meer's back-to-back no-hitters in 1938, as well as Carl Hubbell's 24th straight victory over two seasons (1937) — still a major league record.

A veritable Eighth Wonder of the World!

> *Bat Masterson,*
> Morning Telegraph, *sports editor,*
> *on the Polo Grounds, 1911*

My sons will forever be innocent of the awesome mystery, for a young boy, of the mammoth, mis-shapen, double-tiered, soot-encrusted edifice called the Polo Grounds. They will go through life without ever having explored the secret corners and remote caverns of its interior, without ever having raced and frolicked up and down its innumerable ramps and through its maze of corridors. And without ever having sat in its unique air, a blend of the smoke of 20,000 cigarettes and the aroma of hundreds of gallons of beer gone stale — a mix that compacted and hung like a soggy blanket over the field and gave you a headache by the fourth inning.

> *Thomas Kiernan,*
> *author*

6.

Polo Grounds

The legendary Polo Grounds was a giant of a landmark on the stadium scene, no pun intended. Built in a nestled hollow beneath the cliffs of Coogan's Bluff in northern Manhattan, the massive structure took its near-final form after a fire destroyed the original park in 1911. In the early 1920s, the addition of a covered double-decked grandstand in the shape of a bathtub completed the familiar look of the grounds. The field of play offered shallow foul lines and an expansive breadth of space in center field.

A plethora of magical moments took place there: The Catch by Willie Mays in the '54 World Series, Bobby Thomson's Shot Heard 'Round the World in '51; Christy Mathewson's shutout bonanza in the 1905 World Series; the celebrated Merkle Boner in '08 that eventually cost the Giants the pennant; the death of Cleveland's Ray Chapman, felled by a pitch to the head from Carl Mays in 1920; Carl Hubbell's consecutive fanning of the American League's Big Five in the 1934 All-Star Game, and so many more, not to mention all the classic football episodes that transpired there as well.

In 1958, New Yorkers lost their Giants to San Francisco. Six years later, they lost the venerable Polo Grounds to the same nefarious wrecking ball that had done in Ebbets Field in 1960.

Fenway Park is notoriously booby-trapped. In the left field corner, there is a doorway facing out to the field. When a ball catches the far corner of the doorway, it can carom directly backward, hitting the opposite side of the doorway, which will then bumper-jump the ball to the wall, where it will take yet another carom.

David Falkner,
author

I've seen fielders go nuts because they just didn't know what to do with the wall. They'll try to guess where a ball's going to wind up and instead of going to the ball they'll be standing someplace else looking foolish.

Mike Greenwell,
Boston Red Sox left fielder

The spirit of Babe Ruth has rumbled in historic Fenway Park like the Loch Ness Monster. . .ever since the World Series of 1918, when Ruth won two games. But his departure cast a spell that festered in the crevices and eaves of Fenway. In the dark of night at the Park, the lonely, haunted spirit of the Red Sox howls.

George Vecsey,
sportswriter

5.

Fenway Park

Quaint Fenway Park's unique integration of physical irregularities and eccentricities has endeared itself to generations of old ball park lovers.

The Green Monster, Fenway's 37-foot high, home run-target left field wall, sports the major league's only in-play ladder, which extends from the upper left side of the scoreboard to the top of the Green Monster. Groundskeepers use it to remove batting-practice balls from netting atop the wall.

There's also a marvelous historical link with the past: The infield grass was transplanted to Fenway in 1912, the park's inceptive year, from Boston's hallowed Huntington Avenue Baseball Grounds, which housed the Red Sox from the American League's inaugural season in 1901 through 1911.

The ghosts of not only Ruth but of Jimmie Foxx, Ted Williams, Carl Yastrzemski and Roger Clemens roam Fenway at large, and no greater moment ever rousted the pigeons more than Carlton Fisk's 12th-inning home run to win Game 6 of the 1975 World Series.

An anonymous comment found in Philip Lowry's *Green Cathedrals* describes the almost sacred aura of Fenway: It is a place "where you can sit for hours and feel a serenity that does not exist anywhere else in the world."

If you were in a box seat at Ebbets Field, you were so close you were practically an infielder.

Red Barber

4.
Ebbets Field

Ebbets Field forever stands as the universal memorial to America's timeless love affair with baseball. Fans entering its main-entrance rotunda stepped onto an Italian-marble floor with a baseball-stitch design motif. A massive chandelier hung from the ceiling with 12 arms in the shape of baseball bats, at the end of which were 12 globes representing baseballs.

Erected in 1913, Ebbets Field claimed the most famous right field wall in baseball with its eccentric, concave, concrete facing and wire-screen topping. Few, outside of Brooklyn right fielders Dixie Walker and Carl Furillo, mastered its tricky caroms.

Of course, Ebbets hosted the most famous milestone in baseball history when, on April 15, 1947, Jackie Robinson took the field for the Dodgers. In addition to the legendary moments generated by Mickey Owen and Cookie Lavagetto, no batter in baseball history ever had a bigger day than the Cardinals' Jim Bottomley, who drove in a major-league record 12 RBIs at Ebbets Field against Brooklyn in 1924. It was also the site of big-league baseball's first televised broadcast back in 1939.

The soul of a city and the collective hearts of fans everywhere were walloped when "dem Bums" vacated their shrine for Los Angeles in 1958.

In Wrigley Field, there was this well area in left, and that little area has about an additional forty-five feet, so you really had to know where that fence was. The best way to play it was to position yourself right off the corner of the angle where the wall comes out, so you know that if you turn to your right, you're going to the deep part; if you turn to your left, you're going to the short part.

Ralph Kiner

3.

Wrigley Field

Aesthetically the most pleasing of the three remaining "belles" of ball park antiquity, Chicago's Wrigley Field is the lone surviving park from the pre-World War I Federal League days.

Undoubtedly its most distinguishing characteristic is its famed Boston and Bittersweet ivy-covered outfield walls, planted in 1937 by Bill Veeck. Several stories exist of hit balls getting lost in the draping ivy quagmire, including one World Series episode involving Chicago left fielder Andy Pafko. And Pirates Hall of Famer Roberto Clemente once got ready to rifle — no, not a baseball — but a white soft-drink cup to a relay man on a Cubs extra-base hit!

Wrigley Field was also the site of Babe Ruth's "called-shot" home run in the 1932 World Series and gained a measure of notoriety as baseball's last "day" park, before succumbing to the lights in 1988 — *40 years* after the last of the original 16 major league teams (Detroit) installed lights for night games. It is also where Pete Rose, on September 8, 1985, tied Ty Cobb's all-time hits record.

The saga of Wrigley, thankfully, continues. Its South Side neighbor, Comiskey Park, was a fine old dinosaur itself for 80 years, before giving way to another new-is-better stadium in 1991.

It was as tough a place to play as there was. Not only did you have those angles, but there was also these hooks (on the field-level scoreboard) where they hung those hand-lettered scores. The ball could hit those hooks — and so could you.

Bill Virdon,
Pittsburgh Pirates center fielder,
on Shibe Park

2.

Shibe Park

Philadelphia's Shibe Park opened on April 12, 1909. The centerpiece of its artistic architecture was the homeplate entrance at North 21st and Lehigh — a majestic French Renaissance-inspired dome that once crowned the turreted upper-floor office of Philadelphia Athletics manager Connie Mack.

The park's original dimensions included a daunting, hitter-hostile, 378-foot left field line and a colossal 515 feet to straightaway center. Shibe's infamous right field personified its character: a 12-foot high concrete wall with exposed support beams that enabled balls to take crazy caroms whenever they caught an edge.

Behind the right field wall ran a row of old brownstones on 20th St. that overlooked the fence. For 26 years, people crammed the rooftops and enjoyed the richest of beggars' feasts — a nonpaying seat to the game. That ended in 1935, when Mack erected a 22-foot-high corrugated fence above the original concrete wall, effectively blindfolding the brownstone "bleachers."

On the last day of the 1941 season, Ted Williams put his .400 batting average on the line at Shibe, electing to play a doubleheader and going six-for-eight to wind up at .406.

In 1970, after 33 years as the exclusive domain of the Phillies, the park did its swan song.

It was the biggest one-day show baseball had ever staged...The Yankee tradition of bigness and power began, perhaps, right there that afternoon. Everything was big. The game drew the largest crowd in baseball history — 74,200. (This attendance record stood for 31 years.) The Stadium was the biggest, grandest and tallest baseball park in the world...and on the field in his brand-new white-and-pinstriped uniform was Babe Ruth, the game's biggest star.

> *John Durant,*
> *on Yankee Stadium's opening day,*
> *April 18, 1923*

A ball came off the wall a certain way 30 feet from the foul pole, another way 40 feet from the pole. If you didn't have the angle exactly right, the ball would kick around the wall and be by you for a triple.

> *Charlie "King Kong" Keller,*
> *New York Yankees left fielder (1940-52),*
> *on the Stadium's left field corner*

The fans will soon forget about them over there.

> *Giants manager John McGraw,*
> *on the Yankees move to their new home,*
> *1923*

1.
Old Yankee Stadium

It humbled even the great Ruth. With genuine reverence, The Babe managed to utter, "Some ball yard!"

The majesty and grandeur of the original Yankee Stadium drew ahhhs from every beholder. No venue in baseball history has come close to equaling its flair for the dramatic and its presentation of so many historic moments.

I had your typical Billy Crystal experience; the same introduction to the breathtakingly lush emerald-green playing field after emerging from one of the section/aisle portals as a gawking eight-year-old. Never has there been a ball-park feature anywhere architecturally to rival the Stadium's magnificent upper-deck, copper art-deco frieze facade. Why that was jettisoned in the mid-'70s renovation still begs understanding.

Ruthville, the name for the short right field stands, seductively beckoned to the Sultan for his swats, lying a mere 296 feet down the line from home plate. And then there was Death Valley, that cavernous expanse in left-center that looked like it might be a good three-day hike to traverse. In deepest center field stood the fabled trilogy of monuments — Huggins, Gehrig, Ruth. And yes, I too thought they were all buried there.

Yankee Stadium was given a reprieve and a cheerless facelift after the 1973 season. The best carryover from the old Stadium, however, is a person. Since 1951, the Yankees have had the services of the finest public address announcer in baseball, bar none — a classy, non-hype purveyor of information who perfectly reflects the dignity of the proud and mighty Yankees: Bob Sheppard.

The Stadium's main moments could fill an entire book, but if I had to pick one as the plum it would be Don Larsen's perfect game in the 1956 World Series. Or maybe Roger Maris' 61st home run in 1961...or Al Gionfriddo's catch that robbed DiMaggio in the '47 Series...or Babe Ruth's 60th home run. . .or Sandy Amoros' catch in '55...or...

Traditionalist that I am, I hated to see the beautiful facade go and the fences brought in. In support of John Durant's initial observation of The House, this is one ball park where big should have *stayed* big.

Chapter 8

THE BAT RACK

The Bat Rack

Everything from 30-35 ounces to 33-35 inches in length, some with tar, most custom taped, all thrown into a rack, awaiting the next opportunity for use. In the darkened corners of each cubicle swirl a hundred different superstitions. In the right hands, a bat can change things in an instant. Some have known moments no person or object could describe; moments etched in time — all time. Others sustain cracks, sometimes splitting down the middle, on their first-ever willful swing. Kind of like life. A lot like baseball.

Veeck's Midget Draws Walk, Publicity

Looking to pull people into silent Sportsman's Park to offset longstanding low attendance at St. Louis Browns' games, master showman/promoter/club owner Bill Veeck signs 3-foot, 7-inch midget Eddie Gaedel as a publicity stunt.

On August 19, 1951, facing the Detroit Tigers' Bob Cain in the opening frame of Game 2 of a doubleheader, the 67-pound Gaedel, with an almost non-existent strike zone, draws four straight balls for a walk. A pinch runner is then substituted for Gaedel, but Veeck's outlandish stunt is a success, garnering nationwide publicity.

The Browns lose both games that day, which also marks the American League's golden anniversary. No stunts or gimmicks, though, can keep the Browns from losing 102 games in '51, a distant 46 behind the pennant-winning New York Yankees.

Parking It

Cincinnati's Harry Heilmann, a Hall of Fame slugger, hit home runs in every major league ball park in existence during his career, the first major leaguer to do so.

As a Detroit Tiger, prior to coming to Cincinnati, Heilmann had homered in every American League venue. He nailed the National League parks in his first season with the Reds, in 1930.

Of Babe Ruth's career total of 714 home runs, 708 were hit in the American League, in only nine different ball parks.

By contrast, Henry Aaron, who broke Ruth's mark in early 1974, homered in 23 different parks.

The Lack Thereof

For all their collective achievements that dot the pages of baseball history, neither Babe Ruth nor Hank Aaron ever won a Triple Crown.

Nine Homeless from the Hall

1) Roger Maris
2) Pete Rose
3) Joe Jackson
4) "Smokey Joe" Williams
5) Bob Meusel
6) Tony Perez
7) Ken Boyer
8) Sadaharu Oh
9) Al Rosen

Curt Flood

A seven-time Gold Glove center fielder during his 12 seasons with the St. Louis Cardinals, Curt Flood vowed he'd rather fight than switch, after being traded to the Philadelphia Phillies in 1970. Flood, instead of reporting to Philadelphia, chose to challenge baseball's timeless reserve clause.

Though his efforts were defeated, a similar case five years later involving pitchers Andy Messersmith and Dave McNally ultimately brought about the long-awaited victory for players' freedom.

26-Inning Marathon for Braves, Dodgers in 1920

Playing the equivalent of almost three games in one afternoon, Brooklyn and Boston hooked up at Braves Field, on May 1, 1920, for almost four hours before finally calling it quits after 26 innings and a 1–1 standoff, the longest game in baseball history. Incredibly, both pitchers, Joe Oeschger for the Braves and the Dodgers' Leon Cadore, went the entire distance. It is estimated that they threw in the neighborhood of 250-300 pitches each. The game, which didn't start till 3 P.M., was eventually called because of darkness.

It's amazing that they managed to play 26 innings in under four hours, when the 25-inning Chicago White Sox-Milwaukee Brewers struggle of 1984 took eight hours and six minutes to complete over two days (May 8-9).

1989 — A Tough Year

- Pete Rose is banished from baseball for life.
- Baseball commissioner, A. Bartlett Giamatti, dies of a heart attack one week after exiling Rose from the game.
- A 7.1 earthquake postpones the third game of the World Series between Oakland and San Francisco.

1998 — An Incredible Year

- Mark McGwire's 70 home runs; Sammy Sosa's 66 HRs.
- The New York Yankees 114 wins, an American League record.
- Kerry Wood's 20 Ks in a single game, matches Roger Clemens' all-time mark.
- Rickey Henderson, baseball's all-time base-stealing leader, tops the major leagues, at age 39, with 66 stolen bases.
- Alex Rodriguez becomes only the third player in baseball history to join the exclusive 40-40 Club.
- Cal Ripken Jr. ends his consecutive-game playing streak at 2,632.
- Roger Clemens' unprecedented fifth Cy Young Award.

Mantle Days

There were few boys in '53,
Who didn't wish to be like Mickey.

Fervant youths without exception,
Mirrored the swing of number 7.

Scintillating smooth switch-hitter;
Followed the great Yankee Clipper.

Commerce Comet, swift as a breeze,
Basepaths ablaze on horrible knees.

Mate of Berra, Ford and Skowron,
Woodling, Bauer and Billy Martin.

Bronx Bombers, M & M boys,
The Stadium's rapturous, thunderous noise.

Prodigious shots of sheer raw power,
Past Griffith's and Briggs' light towers.

A deep-bleacher Ballantine blast,
Mel Allen cries, "How 'bout that!"

Legend from a dynasty,
Three-time AL MVP.

'56 triple-crown king,
Seven gold World Series rings.

One of Gotham's Mighty Three:
Duke, The Mick, Say-Hey Willie.

Eighth all-time: career home runs,
Fifty-four in '61.

Ev'ry card collector's ambition:
His '52 Topps in mint condition.

But heroes held too high on shoulders,
Often fall when it's all over.

His final words came truthfully:
"Listen, kids, don't be like me."

We'll not likely soon see his likes,
This classic Yankee in pinstripes.

— Alan Ross

Greatest All-Star Game

1961 — The first of two All-Star Games that year. The swirling wind at Candlestick Park contributed to an All-Star-Game-record seven errors, and no less than *17* future Hall of Famers played in the game: Hank Aaron, Willie Mays, Roberto Clemente, Frank Robinson, Eddie Mathews, Warren Spahn, Stan Musial, Sandy Koufax, Hoyt Wilhelm, Yogi Berra, Mickey Mantle, Whitey Ford, Al Kaline, Jim Bunning, Brooks Robinson, Harmon Killebrew and Nellie Fox. In the bottom of the 10th, Mays doubled in the tying run for the National League and minutes later scored the winning run on Clemente's RBI single to right.

The Merkle Boner

In 1908, the Chicago Cubs forced a playoff against the New York Giants for the National League pennant, when New York's Fred Merkle, in a game against the Cubs near the end of the regular season, failed to touch second base on an apparent Giants game-winning hit.

In the playoff, on October 8, Chicago beat New York behind the clutch pitching of Mordecai "Three Finger" Brown. Though he played solid baseball for another 14 seasons, Merkle never lived down his pennant-losing gaffe.

Lucky No. 13

Brooklyn Dodgers pitcher Ralph Branca, infamous for serving up the "Shot Heard 'Round the World" gopher ball to the New York Giants' Bobby Thomson that decided the 1951 National League pennant, wore No. 13 on his uniform and ironically, also had won 13 games and pitched 13 complete games in that same '51 season — all *before* The Shot!

Have Ball, Will Travel

One of the game's most entertaining stories involves Ernie Lombardi, baseball's likeable "Schnozz" and a 10-year catcher for the Cincinnati Reds in the 1930s and '40s. Lombardi once reportedly parked a home run over Crosley Field's center field wall that landed in the back of a truck traveling on Western Avenue just beyond the fence. From there the ball hitched a ride for 30 miles. The longest homer ever? Lombardi's feat, if not exactly a milestone moment, at the very least qualifies as a mile*age* moment.

40-40 Club

Only three players have ever hit 40 home runs and stolen 40 bases in a season:

- José Canseco, Oakland A's
  (42 homers, 40 stolen bases), 1988
- Barry Bonds, San Francisco Giants
  (42 homers, 40 stolen bases), 1996
- Alex Rodriguez, Seattle Mariners
  (42 homers, 46 stolen bases), 1998

The All-American Girls Baseball League

From 1943 to 1954, while the United States warred globally and then in Korea, the All-American Girls Baseball League was formed to bolster American spirits and supply an entertaining yet skillful grade of baseball for the homeland's hard-core enthusiasts. Organized by Chicago Cubs' owner Philip Wrigley in the fall of 1942, the women's league originally consisted of eight midwestern cities in four states. The girls, in addition to being expected to provide an excellent level of play, were to have "high moral standing" and "femininity was to be stressed at all times."

Former Pittsburgh Pirates Hall of Famer Max Carey, who coached two All-American teams and was League president for five years, said the final game of the 1946 women's championship series was "barring none, even in the majors, the best game I've ever seen."

But the League's death knell sounded in 1954, with the return home from the Korean War of American's male major league stars, as well as the insurgent rise of television.

The Rockford Peaches, the Grand Rapids Chicks, the Racine Belles, et al., soon became just another page, albeit completely unique, in American baseball history.

The 500 Home Run Club

Aaron, Ott, The Babe, The Splendid Splinter, The Mick, Schmidt, Willie — they're all here. But surprisingly, some well-known sluggers did not slug long enough or quite hard enough to join the career elite. Duke Snider, Lou Gehrig, Joe DiMaggio, Hank Greenberg, Stan Musial, Ralph Kiner — all missing from the list. The Fabulous Fifteen:

1.	Hank Aaron	755
2.	Babe Ruth	714
3.	Willie Mays	660
4.	Frank Robinson	586
5.	Harmon Killebrew	573
6.	Reggie Jackson	563
7.	Mike Schmidt	548
8.	Mickey Mantle	536
9.	Jimmie Foxx	534
10.	Ted Williams	521
11.	Willie McCovey	521
12.	Eddie Mathews	512
13.	Ernie Banks	512
14.	Mel Ott	511
15.	Eddie Murray	504

The Bat Rack

When I was a boy growing up in Kansas, a friend of mine and I talked about what we wanted to do when we grew up. I told him I wanted to be a real major league baseball player, a genuine professional like Honus Wagner. My friend said that he'd like to be president of the United States. Neither of us got our wish.

Dwight D. Eisenhower

BIBLIOGRAPHY

&

INDEX

Bibliography

Astor, Gerald. The Baseball Hall of Fame 50th Anniversary Book. New York: Prentice Hall, 1988.

Bak, Richard. Lou Gehrig, An American Classic. Dallas: Taylor Publishing, 1995.

Bjarkman, Peter C., Ed. Encyclopedia of Major League Baseball Team Histories. London, England: Meckler Publishing, 1991.

Bucek, Jeanine, Ed. The Baseball Encyclopedia. 10th edition. New York: Macmillan, 1996.

Chadwick, Bruce. The St. Louis Cardinals. New York: Abbeville Press, 1995.

Cosgrove, Benedict. Covering the Bases. San Francisco, CA: Chroncile Books, 1997.

Dixon, Phil with Patrick Hannigan. The Negro Baseball Leagues. New York: Amereon Ltd., 1992.

Einstein, Charles, Ed. The Fireside Book of Baseball. 4th Edition. New York: Simon & Schuster, 1987.

Falkner, David. Nine Sides of the Diamond. New York: Random House, 1990.

Fimrite, Ron. The World Series. Birmingham, AL: Oxmoor House, Inc., 1993.

Frick, Ford C. Games, Asterisks, and People. New York: Crown Publishers, 1973.

Grayson, Harry. They Played the Game. New York: A.S. Barnes and Company, 1944, 1945.

Gutman, Dan. The Way Baseball Works. New York: Simon & Schuster, 1996.

Honig, Donald. Baseball in the '50s. New York: Crown Publishers, Inc., 1987.

James, Bill. The Bill James Historical Baseball Abstract. New York: Villard Books, 1986.

Johnson, Susan E. When Women Played Baseball. Seattle, WA: Seal Press, 1994.

Karst, George and Martin J. Jones, Jr. Who's Who in Professional Baseball. New York: Arlington House, 1973.

Kiernan, Thomas. The Miracle of Coogan's Bluff. New York: Thomas Y. Crowell Company, 1975.

Lieb, Fred. Baseball As I Have Known It. New York: Coward, McCann & Geoghegan, Inc., 1977.

Lowry, Philip J. Green Cathedrals. Reading, MA: Addison-Wesley Publishing Co., 1992.

Nemec, David. Great Baseball Feats, Facts & Firsts. New York: Penguin Books, 1987.

Okkonen, Marc. Baseball Memories. New York: Sterling Press, 1992.

Osborne, Charles, Ed. Yesterday in Sport. New York: Time-Life Books, 1968.

Reichler, Joe, Ed. The Game & the Glory. New Jersey: Prentice-Hall, 1976.

Reidenbaugh, Lowell. Baseball's Greatest Games. St. Louis, MO: The Sporting News, 1986.

Rhodes, Greg and John Erardi. Crosley Field. Cincinnati, OH: Road West Publishing, 1995.

Ritter, Lawrence S. Lost Ballparks. New York: Viking, 1992.

Smith, John, Ed. 1997 Official Major League Baseball Fact Book. St. Louis, MO: The Sporting News Publishing Company, 1997.

Smith, Ken. Baseball's Hall of Fame. New York: Grosset and Dunlap. 1952.

Sullivan, Dean A., Ed. Early Innings. University of Nebraska Press, 1995.

Thorn, John and Peter Palmer, Michael Gershman, David Pietrusza. Total Baseball. 5th edition. New York: Viking Press, 1997.

Verducci, Tom. "The Greatest Season Ever." Sports Illustrated. 5 October 1998: 38-52.

Wallace, Joseph, Ed. The Baseball Anthology. New York: Harry N. Abrams, 1994.

Ward, Geoffrey and Ken Burns. Baseball An Illustrated History. New York: Alfred C. Knopf: New York, 1994.

Index

About the Author

Sports historian and writer Alan Ross lives in Monteagle, Tennessee. A graduate of Fordham University, he is a former editor for Professional Team Publications, Athlon Sports Communications, and Walnut Grove Press. His feature articles on sports history have appeared in *The Sporting News*, *Lindy's*, *Athlon Sports*, *Athletic Administration*, *Game Day*, *NFL Insider*, *Arizona Cardinals Media Guide,* and *Track Record*. In addition, Ross is the history columnist for *Oilers Exclusive*, the official publication of the NFL's Tennessee Oilers. He has authored four other books, *A Brief History of Golf, Golf à la cart, Hooked on Hockey* and a non-sports book, *Love Is Forever,* co-written with his wife, Karol.

If you enjoyed this book, you're sure to enjoy other sports-related titles from Walnut Grove Press. For more information about books on golf, baseball, football, basketball, hockey, tennis and stock car racing, please call:
1-800-256-8584